Birthplace of R

Sketch, by J. R. Brown of the S&D Railway opening

This guide is a celebration of a remarkable decade in Stockton's history, a decade which saw a thriving Georgian market town and busy port transform itself into the focal point of a worldwide transport revolution.

Railways — with their fast, cheap carriage of raw materials and finished goods, not to mention people and ideas — were perhaps the single most important factor in the emergence of Britain, by the mid 19th century, as the world's first major industrialised nation. But it was in North East England, and in Stockton-on-Tees in particular, that an event took place in the 1820s which, more than any other, was to capture the imagination of people throughout Britain and Western Europe. The opening of the Stockton and Darlington Railway, the world's first commercially successful public railway, took place on September 27, 1825, and led directly to the Railway Revolution. More than a century and a half later, there is still much to be seen in and around the Borough of Stockton on Tees which recalls that remarkable decade when the railway was planned, built and first operated.

This unique story is to be found within the very fabric of the town itself. This booklet pieces together part of that story using the buildings and surroundings of Stockton as a backcloth.

Old Stockton is still waiting to be explored. Though modern development has replaced the old crowded port and rail terminal by the Tees, and the railway no longer follows its original course near the town centre, much still survives to provide a real insight into what made Stockton "the birthplace of railways".

The Story of The Stockton and Darlington Railway

"Now lads, I venture to tell you that I think you will live to see the day when the railway will supercede almost all other methods of conveyance in this country.....the time is coming when it will be cheaper for a working man to travel upon a railway than to walk on foot."

George Stephenson

The Stockton and Darlington Railway proved to the world that a steam-hauled passenger and freight service could be an efficient and profitable reality: it became both the inspiration and the blueprint for all future railway companies. The widely publicised success of the S&D marked the real beginning of the Railway Age, that great symbol of Victorian success and prosperity. Yet the opening of the line in 1825 was merely the culmination of well over a century's technical development and constant experimentation.

The idea and concept of a "rail" way was familiar even in the 17th century and widely practised in the 18th century, in mines and quarries. By using horses to drag bulky raw materials along regular runs, originally made from wood and later from cast iron, friction and drag could be reduced and much larger quantities of material could be moved at lower costs. These wagonways or primitive tramways were rarely more than a few miles in length, often connecting the mines to the nearest navigable waterway. Early tramways are found all over the British Isles, particularly in mining districts like Cornwall, Yorkshire, South Wales and Durham; one of the largest and most important networks of all was developed to serve the Northumberland and Durham coalfield. More than 20 years before *Locomotion No.1* was built, there had been numerous experiments with stationary steam engines and steam

Trevithick's Engine, 1803

Hedley's Puffing Billy, 1813

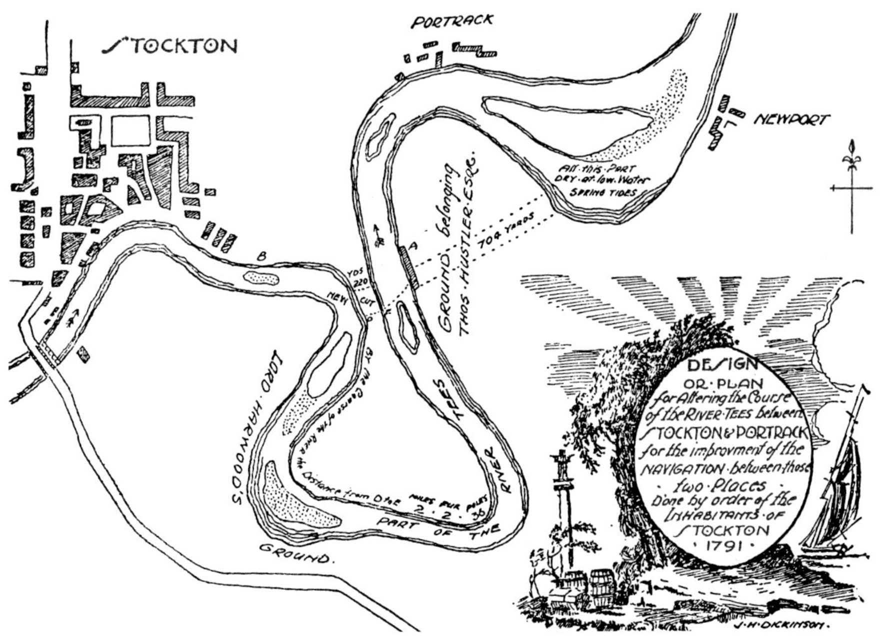

Design for the new cut between Portrack and Stockton

locomotive haulage. In 1804 Trevithick's primitive engine hauled 25 tons on Penydarren tramway at Merthyr Tydfil, and later there was Hedley's *Puffing Billy* (1813) and Blenkinsop's remarkable engines at Middleton Colliery, near Leeds.

George Stephenson (1781-1848) learned his trade in the mining industry of Tyneside, and soon had a national reputation for his work as an enginewright at Killingworth Colliery, building and constantly improving the design of steam locomotives which were attracting curiosity and attention throughout Europe.

How did the prosperous little port of Stockton come to get itself involved with this remarkable personality and his bold experiments in iron horses and railroads?

It all began as far back as 1810, at a celebratory dinner in Stockton's Town House (Town Hall) to mark the opening of the "New Cut" between Portrack and Stockton (a length of canalised river designed to remove an awkward bend in the River Tees). At this dinner, Leonard Raisbeck, Stockton's Recorder, successfully moved a resolution that a committee be appointed to enquire into the practicality and advantage of a railway or canal from Stockton to Darlington and Winston.

At the beginning of the 19th century, Stockton was already an important commercial centre and busy port with a well established trade in lead and farm produce. It was therefore not surprising that the town's entrepreneurial spirit saw the advantage of breaking the monopoly

George Stephenson

established by the wealthy colliery owners of the Tyne hinterland. These mines were very deep and dipped towards the sea, but coal could easily be moved by short wagonways to the navigable Rivers Tyne and Wear. In contrast, the coalfields around Bishop Auckland in County Durham were easier to mine, but almost inaccessible without huge transport costs — unless, of course, a canal or railway could be built linking these rich coal seams to the towns of Darlington and Yarm, and the port of Stockton.

Schemes had already been suggested before this date; indeed James Brindley and his assistant Whitworth surveyed a canal in 1768, as did Ralph Todd in 1796, but both projects had to be abandoned owing to the expense and a shortage of money. By 1812, there were two rival groups of promoters, one proposing a canal, and the other a tramroad. The debate was finally resolved in favour of a railway which surveys suggested would be cheaper and more practical than a canal.

However, it was the Quakers who proved to be of special importance to the idea of a Stockton and Darlington Railway, particularly one Edward Pease (1767-1856), a Darlington woollen merchant and banker. Not only did he adamantly believe that a railway would be the best solution, but he was able to persuade fellow Quakers in Norwich (the Gurneys) and London (Richardson's banking firm) to provide the badly needed investment capital, and additional loans to ensure the railway became a reality.

The Stockton and Darlington

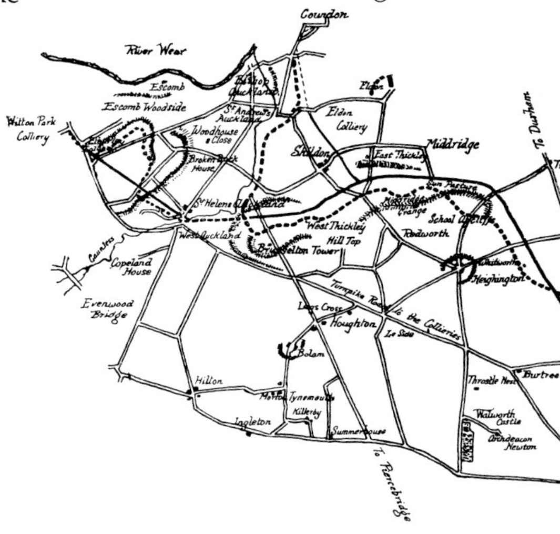

Railway has often been nicknamed the *Quaker railway*, reflecting the amount of drive and energy Pease and his friends were to contribute to its development. After the railway plan finally received Royal Assent in 1821, it was Pease, unhappy with the original route surveyed by George Overton, who secured the services of George Stephenson for an alternative survey. Stephenson's route was three miles shorter than Overton's, passed nearer to Darlington and was considerably cheaper to build, at £64,640.

On January 22, 1822, Stephenson was formally appointed Engineer to the project at an annual salary of £660. Construction began on May 23, 1822, when — to the peal of church bells — Thomas Meynell of Yarm, Chairman of the Railway Company, accompanied by the Mayor, the Recorder and Members of Stockton Corporation, cut the first sod and laid the first rail at St John's Well, at what is now Bridge Road.

Locomotion No. 1

...LINGTON RAILWAY
... Stephenson's Alterations

Durham County Council Library

The track was constructed on 4' $8^{1}/_{2}$" gauge, a size now used worldwide, and chosen by Stephenson because he had used it for his railway at Killingworth Colliery — reputedly because it corresponded to the standard width of Roman carts. Most of the line was built from 15-foot malleable wrought iron rails, rather than cast iron, which was more liable to fracture. Unlike modern railway track, the rails were not connected by the sleepers: each ran on a separate line of sleepers. On the western part of the route, the rails were set on stone blocks quarried locally, and nearer Stockton, from oak timbers cut from old ships being broken up at Portsmouth, sold off cheap at six old pence a timber !

It was Stephenson who

persuaded the S & D to operate steam locomotives rather than use horse traction, and the Act of 1823 authorised both their use and Stephenson's new route. In May 1824 Edward Pease and his cousin Thomas Richardson entered into partnership with George Stephenson and his 19-year-old son Robert (also to become a great railway engineer) to establish the locomotive building company of Robert Stephenson & Co, Newcastle. In September two locomotives — *Locomotion* and *Hope* were ordered from the new company at a cost of £500 each.

THE

STOCKTON & DARLINGTON

RAILWAY COMPANY

Hereby give Notice,

THAT the FORMAL OPENING of their RAILWAY will take place on the 27th instant, as announced in the public Papers.—The Proprietors will assemble at the Permanent Steam Engine, situated below BRUSSELTON TOWER*, *about nine Miles West of* DARLINGTON, *at 8 o'clock, and, after examining their extensive inclined Planes there, will start from the Foot of the* BRUSSELTON *descending Plane, at 9 o'clock, in the following Order:—*

1. THE COMPANY'S LOCOMOTIVE ENGINE.
2. The ENGINE'S TENDER, with Water and Coals.
3. SIX WAGGONS, laden with Coals, Merchandize, &c.
4. The COMMITTEE, and other PROPRIETORS, in the COACH belonging to the COMPANY.
5. SIX WAGGONS, with Seats reserved for STRANGERS.
6. FOURTEEN WAGGONS, for the Conveyance of Workmen and others.

☞ *The WHOLE of the above to proceed to STOCKTON.*

7. SIX WAGGONS, laden with Coals, to leave the Procession at the DARLINGTON BRANCH.
8. SIX WAGGONS, drawn by Horses, for Workmen and others.
9. Ditto Ditto.
10. Ditto Ditto.
11. Ditto Ditto.

The COMPANY'S WORKMEN to leave the Procession at DARLINGTON, and DINE at that Place at ONE o'clock; excepting those to whom Tickets are specially given for YARM, and for whom Conveyances will be provided, on their Arrival at STOCKTON.

TICKETS will be given to the Workmen who are to dine at DARLINGTON, specifying the Houses of Entertainment.

The PROPRIETORS, and such of the NOBILITY and GENTRY as may honour them with their Company, will DINE precisely at THREE o'clock, at the TOWN-HALL, STOCKTON.—Such of the Party as may incline to return to DARLINGTON that Evening, will find Conveyances in waiting for their Accommodation, to start from the COMPANY'S WHARF there precisely at SEVEN o'clock.

The COMPANY take this Opportunity of enjoining on all their WORK-PEOPLE that Attention to *Sobriety* and *Decorum* which they have hitherto had the Pleasure of observing.

The COMMITTEE give this PUBLIC NOTICE, that all Persons who shall ride upon, or by the sides of, the RAILWAY, on Horseback, will incur the Penalties imposed by the Acts of Parliament passed relative to this RAILWAY.

* Any Individuals desirous of seeing the Train of Waggons descending the inclined Plane from ETHERLEY, and in Progress to BRUSSELTON, may have an Opportunity of so doing, by being on the RAILWAY at ST. HELEN'S AUCKLAND not later than Half-past Seven o'clock.

RAILWAY-OFFICE, *Sept. 19th*, 1825.

ATKINSON's Office, High-Row, Darlington

Press notice announcing the opening of the railway

SEPTEMBER 27, 1825 — The Railway Age is Born

A notice appeared in the press announcing that the Stockton and Darlington Railway would open on September 27, 1825, and ambitious celebrations were planned, with open invitations given to the region's nobility and landed gentry, to travel along the 25 mile route from Etherly to Stockton, where they would enjoy a grand banquet at the Town House.

There was a great deal of excitement and interest surrounding the opening day. A huge crowd gathered before dawn, at the start of the route at the collieries near Shildon, to watch the wagons of coal being hoisted up the two inclines at Etherley and Brussleton by the new stationary winding engines. Waiting at the Mason's Arms Crossing in Shildon was *Locomotion No.1*, and the coach, *Experiment*. It must have been an impressive sight, with George Stephenson and his brother James on the footplate of the brightly painted six-ton loco (it was only later that it was painted in a more sober brown pigment). Timothy Hackworth, the newly appointed Railway Superintendent, acted as guard and he and Stephenson and the brakemen wore blue sashes, while all the other company workmen wore blue ribbons in their button- holes. The atmosphere must have been electric with anticipation, and perhaps apprehension. A contemporary report in the *Durham County Advertiser* describes the "JohnnyRaws" (country folk) running away the first time the engine let off steam as they feared an explosion was imminent.

The coach Experiment Illustrated London News

In front of more than 40,000 spectators along the route, *Locomotion* hauled the coach *Experiment* and 38 wagons, far more than was originally intended, with more than 300 people aboard, and as the journey continued, more crowded on until the number rose to more than 600. The *Experiment* had cost £80 to build, and was really a grander version of a road stage coach, carpeted and red cushioned, though unsprung. Its side- facing seats could hold between 16 and18 passengers and it was here that local celebrities and bigwigs were carried in style, compared with the rough open chauldron or coal wagons used for the other passengers.

It took two hours to complete the nine-mile journey between Shildon and Darlington, but this included stops to remove a defective wagon and a stray piece of oakum that had managed to get into one of *Locomotion's* waterfeed pipes. Allowing for that, the journey time was in effect 65 minutes, with average speeds of around eight miles per hour. At Darlington, the six wagons containing coal were unloaded and distributed to the poor of the parish, and at Yarm Junction a brass band joined the train.

A famous story based on eyewitness accounts relates that on the descent into Stockton, Stephenson gave the engine its head and the train supposedly reached an amazing 15 miles per hour. It is doubtful whether the engine would actually have withstood such speed for any length of time, the smoke box reportedly glowing red hot. Where the new railway ran parallel with the turnpike road (quite possibly in the vicinity of Preston Park), a four-horsed stagecoach is reputed to have raced the train, and though versions vary as to who won the day, the contrast between a transport mode capable of carrying a maximum of 16 passengers, compared with one capable of hauling more than 600, demonstrated the superiority of the new technology for all to see.

Locomotion arrived in Stockton at 3.45 in the afternoon to be greeted by cheers, the national anthem and a 21-gun salute: in such spectacular fashion was the Railway Age born.

The Next Ten Years

Despite the successful opening of the railway, there were many problems for the company to solve — not least of which were the huge financial loans which needed speedy repayment. But the more pressing task was the daily running of an enterprise with few technical and commercial precedents.

Initially the S&D only had *Locomotion No 1* available in service , and though by 1827 it had three sister engines — *Hope, Black Diamond* and *Diligence* — they were never very reliable. A fifth engine, *Chittaprat,* was commissioned in 1827, but this was never fully operational. Even if they had been more reliable, these locomotives were inadequate to meet the demand. Therefore, in the early years, horses were used for much of the freight, andon all passenger services.

The whole construction of the line had, in fact, been designed to facilitate the free passage of horses with no linking sleepers across the trackbed. Though the track was often much drier than the roads of the day, there were still problems, particularly in the downhill sections of the line, where a train of four chauldron waggons had a tendency to overrun the animal.

The problem was eventually solved in 1828 with the construction of a "Dandy cart" — a small wagon which was attached to the rear of the train in which the horse could ride downhill and perhaps eat fodder while the train was controlled by the brake. This enabled the Stockton & Darlington to get 240 miles a week from its horses, compared with 164 miles previously, and haul 12 tons of coal per journey. In comparison, a pre-railway age packhorse could only carry half a ton on its back, so even with horse power the railway could still provide considerable savings.

The fact remained that it was 30 per cent cheaper to haul trains even by unreliable steam locomotives, than by horses. In 1827, Timothy Hackworth, Stephenson's Superintendent, totally rebuilt engine No 5, and in so doing produced the first really successful and reliable locomotive — the *Royal George.* Much more powerful and rugged than its predecessors, it was soon hauling 23 coal wagons or 46½ tons

Locomotion No. 1 painted by JohnWigston

Trustees of the Science Museum

A Stephenson family group — George, holding an oil lamp, is looking at his son Robert

Chauldron wagon

and travelling more than 36 miles a day. It was much larger and heavier than any previous engine, and proved a prototype for a series of highly successful Hackworth machines which were to give decades of excellent service, and establish the supremacy of steam locomotives over horse power.

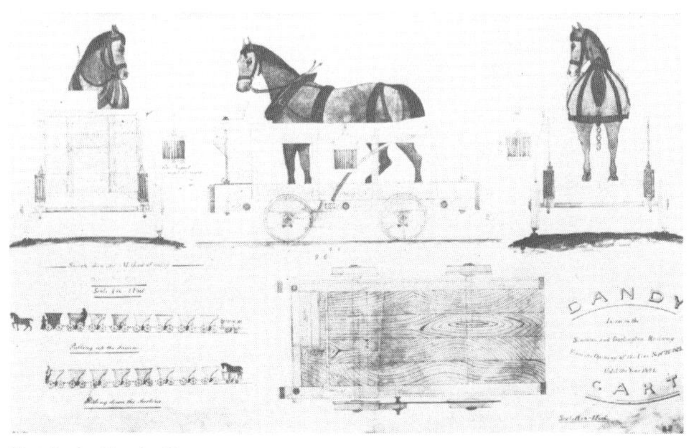

Sketch of a Dandy Cart

The growth in freight traffic on the line soon indicated that the company's 150 chauldron wagons were insufficient. In the first three months of operation, 10,000 tons of coal were carried as well as iron ore, lime, timber, lead and general merchandise. However, the railway had been set up on the same legal basis as a canal company or turnpike trust with its original purpose to provide a thoroughfare upon which others beside the company could use their wagons for the payment of an agreed toll. This proved extremely profitable.

It was only in 1826 that the first ship, the *Adamant*, was loaded with coal at Stockton wharves and trade really began to expand. Four staithes were built by 1827 and 19,448 tons of coal were exported in 1828. An extension of the line across the Tees to what was to become the new port and town of Middlesbrough was opened on December 27, 1830. Again this was a project sponsored by the Pease family wishing to build a rival to well-established coastal ports like Sunderland. The dramatic growth and success of Middlesbrough — ironically soon to rival and overtake Stockton as a port — was the direct result of the Stockton and Darlington Railway.

On October 10, 1825, the first regular S&D horse-drawn passenger services began. The original *Experiment* coach proved unpopular with the travelling public, so the Company went back to a more conventional coach style, though retaining the name.

Initially, passenger services were little more than an afterthought to the main business of freight carriage.

The journey between Stockton and Darlington took two hours, trains running daily except on Sundays, and passengers were charged one shilling a mile, (equivalent to several pounds at present day values). The service proved popular and a second coach *Express* was run to provide a faster and improved service. Other operators soon went into competition — usually inn-keepers whose premises were close to the railway, exactly like traditional stage-coach operators along turnpike roads — to and from roadside inns where tickets were sold. These operators included Martha Howson from the Black Lion, Stockton, with the *Defence* and *Defiance* and Richard Scott of the Kings Head, Darlington who operated *Union*. Within 15 months of opening, seven regular coaches, covering 45,450 miles annually, carried between three and four thousand passengers and earned £503 in fares.

RAPID, SAFE, AND CHEAP TRAVELLING

By the Elegant NEW RAILWAY COACH,

THE UNION,

Which will COMMENCE RUNNING on the STOCKTON and DARLINGTON RAILWAY, on MONDAY the 16th day of October, 1826,

And will call at Yarm, and pass within a mile of Middleton Spa, on its way from Stockton to Darlington, and *vice versa*.

FARES. Inside $1\frac{1}{2}$d.—Outside, 1d. per Mile. Parcels in proportion.

No gratuities expected by the Guard or Coachman.

N. B. The Proprietors will not be accountable for any Parcel of more than £5. value, unless entered and paid for accordingly.

The UNION will run from the Black Lion Hotel and New Inn, Stockton, to the New Inn, Yarm, and to the Black Swan Inn, near the Croft Branch, Darlington; at each of which Inns passengers and parcels are booked, and the times of starting may be ascertained, as also at the Union Inn, Yarm, and Talbot Inn, Darlington.

On the 19th and 20th of October, the Fair Days at Yarm, the Union will leave Darlington at six in the morning for Yarm, and will leave Yarm for Darlington again at six in the evening; in the intermediate time, each day, it will ply constantly between Stockton and Yarm, leaving each place every half hour.

The Union railway coach

There was no formal signalling system but a complicated code of

practice evolved, goods trains giving precedence to coaches at passing loops — a system not always without risk and confusion.

The growing success of the passenger services finally convinced the company of the importance of passengers on the railway, rather than just the carriage of goods which had been the main reason for building the line. In 1833, the S&D took over the operation of all services and began its own regular steam-hauled passenger trains between the two towns six times a day, exploiting the greater speed and carrying capacity of Hackworth's new engines.

The success of the Stockton and Darlington Railway was a remarkable tribute to the vision and foresight of its early promoters, many of them leading Stockton and Yarm personalities. But it was not just a great pioneering engineering achievement; the S&D had proved how railways could be an outstanding commercial success.

The accounts ending June 30, 1826 showed a $2\frac{1}{2}$ per cent dividend to shareholders, which by the late 1830s had risen to between 12 per cent and 15 per cent — an excellent return on capital investment. Pease had

The Royal George painted by John Wigston

Darlington Borough Council

John Dobbin's painting of the opening of the S&D

only promised 5 per cent.

That more than anything else brought about the boom in railway building and development which was soon to transform Britain into the world's first industrial nation.

S&D railway share certificate

THE

Stockton & Darlington Railway Company.

CLASS A PREFERENTIAL 5 PER CENT SHARES.

No. 15415 £25 Share

This is to Certify that [illegible] Kent, Merchant, [illegible] Cumberland, and Charles John [illegible], of No. 12, Eaton Place, Middlesex, Esquire, are the Proprietors of the CLASS A PREFERENTIAL SHARE Numbered 15415 in the STOCKTON & DARLINGTON RAILWAY COMPANY, subject to the Rules Regulations and Orders of the said Company.

Given under the Common Seal of the said Company. Dated the Twenty Fourth day of September in the year of our Lord one thousand eight hundred & fifty eight.

[illegible] Secretary

Courtesy of The Northern Echo

The Stockton BIRTHPLACE OF RAILWAYS Trail

To explore all that there is to see and do linked to the Birthplace of Railways in Stockton Borough will require a whole day or, preferably, two.

We have divided the Trail into two parts.

First is a walk around Stockton itself, looking at some surviving buildings and important sites in and around the town.

The second will require either your own transport or public transport (train or bus) to look at a number of sites out of town. The advantage of using the train in particular is that part of the present day railway in Stockton Borough — British Rail's Heritage Line — still uses the exact line of the Stockton and Darlington Railway, but you must be prepared to walk some distance from the stations. There are frequent local bus services to shorten the journey.

PART ONE
Stockton Town

Begin at the Stockton Tourist Information Centre in Theatre Yard — easily reached by following the signs off High Street near the Town Hall or off Finkle Street.

Theatre Yard

The first part of the Trail gives a glimpse of pre-railway Stockton, and there is no better place to start than in Stockton's Theatre Yard within a fascinating enclosed area of old buildings and yards. This was once part of the complex pattern of narrow riverside alleys and old warehouses, typical of any port, leading off the spacious High Street. The surviving buildings date from the 18th century, Stockton's heyday as an important port on the tidal River Tees. They are situated at the highest point on the river that larger cargo-carrying vessels could reach, though smaller vessels (to save expensive packhorse and road waggon costs) went as far as Yarm.

Daniel Defoe, in his travels through Yorkshire and Durham in the 1720s described Stockton and "Yarum" as "two good towns" which had "greatly increased of late years, especially the first, by being the chiefest place in the North Riding of York or in the county of Cumberland for the shipping of lead, and butter for London".

The stonework from the original medieval castle of Stockton has been incorporated into some of the buildings in and around the yard.

Theatre Yard

Green Dragon Museum

The museum is housed within a Georgian warehouse in Theatre Yard, adjacent to the Information Centre, with collections and displays devoted to the history of Stockton; the old wine cellar also contains a collection of local pottery. Of particular interest is a detailed scale model of St. John's Crossing and the Stockton and Darlington Railway as it used to be, the site of which, will be visited later on the Trail. There is also a section of the original track and a model of a S&D guard in replica railway uniform which has been recreated from an original painting in the National Railway Museum — the earliest railway uniform livery to have survived.

The Georgian Theatre

The nearby Georgian theatre — one of few theatres to have survived in England from this period and the oldest known — was originally a tithe barn belonging to the Bishop of Durham. The theatre opened in 1766, but closed 1866, re-opening in 1874 as Salvation Army premises; it was later used as a sweet factory. In 1980 it was renovated and is now a favourite venue of local dramatic groups. There is a small exhibition of Stockton theatrical history inside which can be seen when the building is open.

Turn left by the Cottage Teashop, and left under the archway into Wasp Nest Yard.

Wasp Nest Yard

Now rebuilt as a pleasant court yard this too was part of the labyrinth of alleys and yards, housing a huge number of families, often in extremely squalid conditions. Beneath the surface are many water cisterns that once served local inhabitants. It was only with the gradual introduction of paving and pure piped water that the continual cycle of cholera epidemics were eliminated in the mid 19th century.

Turn right down Silver Street. Go left at the bottom along Cross Street and across into Bishop Street (north).

Silver Street and the Lead Trade

The lead trade made Stockton an important trading centre and port in the 18th and 19th centuries. It was from here that the large companies like the London (Quaker) Lead Company sent the lead mined in Swaledale and Teesdale to the capital. Many thousands of fodders of lead (and ounces of silver) were carried, along Silver Street, to waiting sailing ships at the Bishop's

The Stockton
BIRTHPLACE OF RAILWAYS
Trail Map

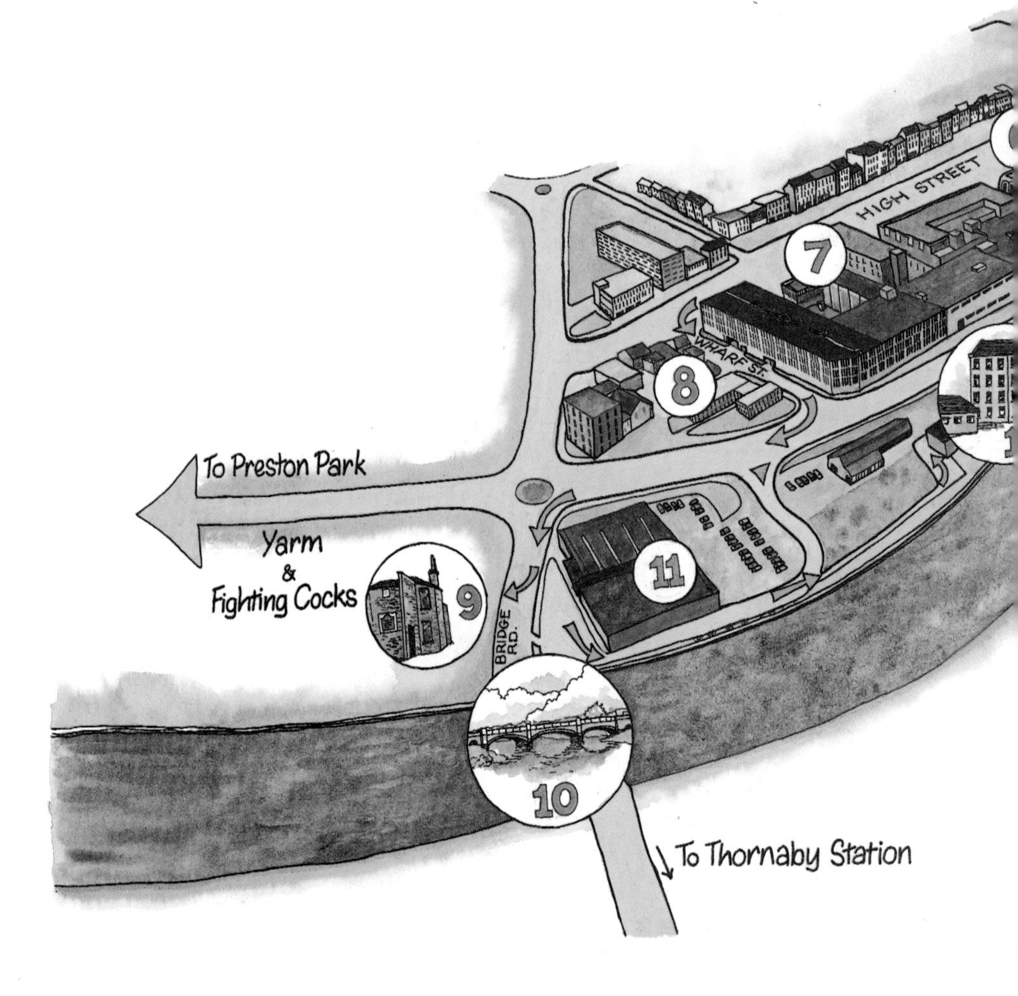

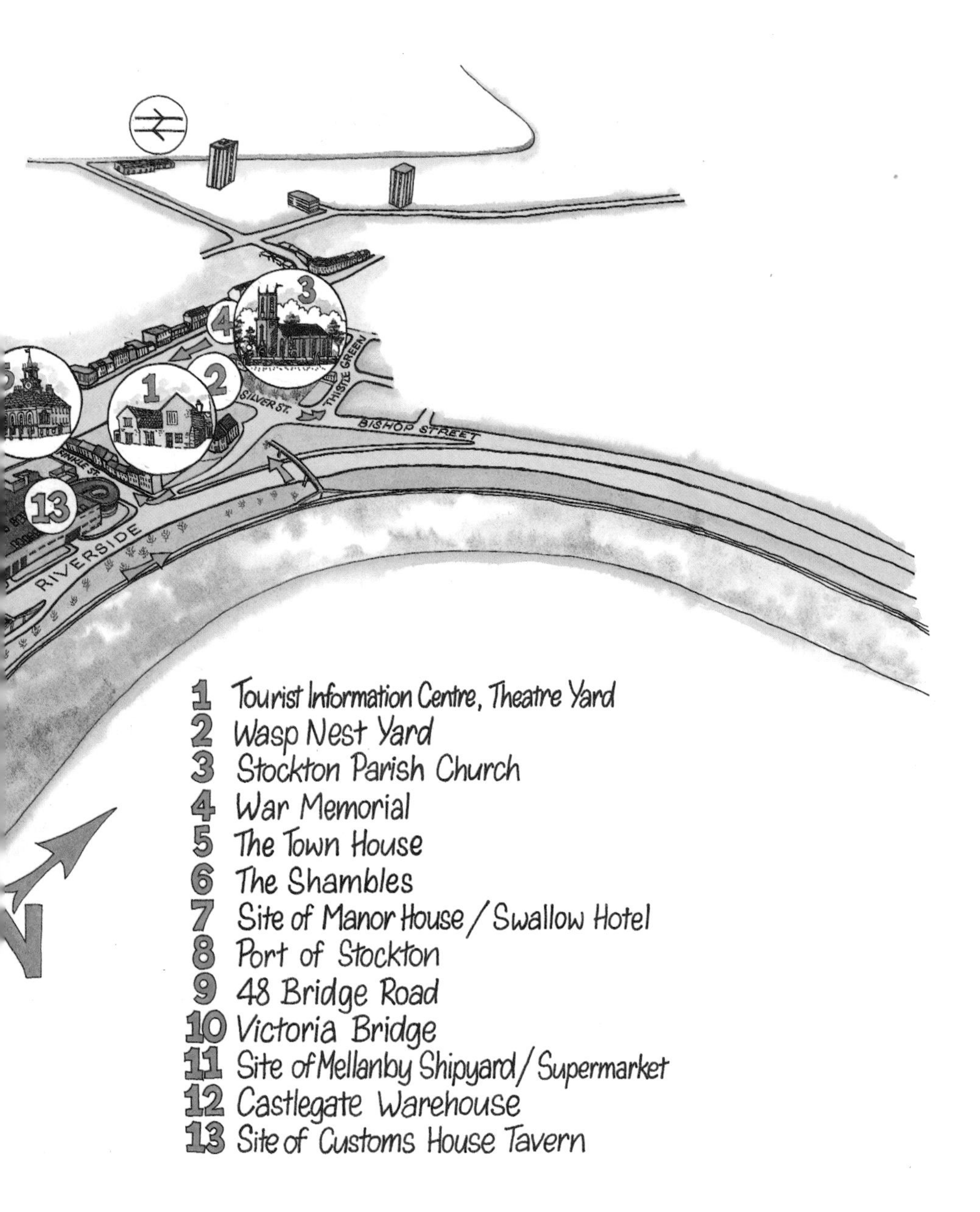
SILVER ST.
THISTLE GREEN
BISHOP STREET
RIVERSIDE
1 Tourist Information Centre, Theatre Yard
2 Wasp Nest Yard
3 Stockton Parish Church
4 War Memorial
5 The Town House
6 The Shambles
7 Site of Manor House / Swallow Hotel
8 Port of Stockton
9 48 Bridge Road
10 Victoria Bridge
11 Site of Mellanby Shipyard / Supermarket
12 Castlegate Warehouse
13 Site of Customs House Tavern

Landing Place. Originally the lead was taken by packhorse from the smelt mills in Arkengarthdale and Swaledale to Richmond where another set of carriers with wagons completed the journey to Stockton and sent it by coastal shipping to London·where it was used for roofing and piping. It is said that many major public buildings and churches are still roofed with Durham and Yorkshire lead.

Turn left and walk up Thistle Green.

Thistle Green

This street again was once lined with tumble-down houses and cottages but they have now been replaced by a police station, a library and municipal buildings.

Left into the Church Yard. Enter the Church by either the side or front door.

Stockton Parish Church

The Church yard was once the site of a medieval Chapel-of-Ease dedicated to Thomas à Becket (1235). The staircase in the present church is of medieval origin and couldhave come from the old chapel. The dedication was dropped in 1538, after Henry VIII denounced Becket's martyrdom and declared him a traitor. It became known as the OldChurch.

Until 1713 Stockton was in the parish of Norton, a nearby village, and its establishment as a separate parish illustrates the town's growth in importance by the 18th century. It was Thomas Rudd (Vicar of Norton and Curate of Stockton in 1705) who championed Stockton's rise in status, and started a subscription from among local wealthy merchants to build its own parish church. The Church was completed in 1712, its size and grandeur reflecting the town's prosperity at the time. It has been claimed that the Church was designed by Wren, but the only evidence to support this has been proved a forgery.

It is a beautiful and elegant church, and it is difficult to imagine that it once contained huge galleries to accommodate a large congregation. These were removed in the 1890s and sadly in 1906 the pulpit was reduced from a typical 18th century "triple decker" to a double decker. The Chancel was also added in 1906 to "Wrenify" the church and the Lady Chapel dates from 1925.

The Church, earlier this century

It is believed that the Communion rails and Holy Table are made from the oak salvaged from Captain Cook's *Endeavour*, and presented by Captain Christopher, who accompanied Cook on his third trip round the world and was later the Commodore of Hudson Bay in Canada. The story has never been substantiated and another story claims they are carved from drift wood picked up on one of Cook's voyages.

The carved pew heads are particularly interesting, each one being different. There is one dedicated to John Walker, the local chemist who invented the friction match in 1826, and on the left, opposite the third pillar, is one commemorating the centenary of the Stockton and Darlington Railway, showing *Locomotion No.1*, and *Experiment*.

But of particular interest is the memorial to Leonard Raisbeck, who first proposed the idea of a railway for Stockton in 1810.

Once out of the church, turn left past the splendid War Memorial by the main gate and continue along the High Street.

The High Street

The long, broad High Street is typical of a North Yorkshire or South Durham market town, being reputedly the widest in England, evidence of Stockton's prosperity and importance since Georgian times. Since 1310 Stockton has played host to a colourful street market. It is now the region's biggest and is held every Wednesday and

Above: Stockton High Street in the 1890s and, below, how it looks today

A busy market day in Stockton

Finkle Street, Stockton where the town's oldest house can be found

Above: Pew end, Stockton Parish Church, commemorating the S&D's centenary Below: Plaque, Bridge Road, marking the laying of the first section of track

Above: Yarm Parish Church which dates mainly from the 18th century. Right: Yarm Town Hall, built in 1710 as a courthouse and market hall.

Above: Preston Hall
Inset: A reconstruction of the type of street that might have been found in any north-eastern town in the 1890s, inside Preston Hall Museum.

Saturday (with a smaller one on Fridays).

It is well worth spending a little time tracing some of the impressive Georgian facades above the modern day shop fronts. Look for the carved ship on the right hand side almost opposite the Town Hall.

Nearby at no. 104 is the birthplace of John Walker, the inventor of the friction match. Also on the right is Ropery Street which, as the name suggests, contained a rope works which produced many of the coils of rope required in the port. The High Street was once full of inns frequented by the many sailors.

There were also several coaching inns, Stockton being on the main stage coach routes between Yorkshire and Edinburgh and Newcastle and London. The inn trade reached its peak in the 1820s and 1830s immediately prior to the coming of the railways as a national network which soon destroyed the stagecoach system.

Continue to the Town House and Shambles.

The Town House

Stockton is justly proud of the fact that it was one of the original Incorporated Boroughs created by the Municipal Corporations Act of 1835. The Town House is one of the ten oldest municipal buildings in Britain that are still in use for their original purpose.

The Town House has an interesting history. In medieval times it was originally a small thatched cottage in the market place in which rents, tolls, prerequisites, fines and admittance to the market were paid. After the Restoration (1660) a purpose-built stone tollbooth was built next to the cottage. It would have had a small lock up, or jail for both serious and minor offences such as drunkenness. It was also used as a temporary jail for those who had escaped hanging, but awaited exile to the American plantations.

The cottage was also used as a butcher's and then as a smithy at the modest annual rent of four old pence. However, by the early 18th century, Stockton was growing in importance and it was decided in 1735 to build the present handsome Town House, at a cost of £513 11s. In 1743, plans were made to extend the building onto the site of the tollbooth.

Like the tollbooth, the new Town House had a jail under the stairs and it continued to be the town's lock-up till 1851 and the building of the police station. In typical 18th century style, a six-column piazza was built on the north side in 1768,

The Town House about 1865

which was replaced in 1900 by an iron canopy. Sadly this too disappeared to help the War effort in 1939.

At the south side door the Serjeant at Mace would have collected rents for the Corporation, and attended the market. There were shops on the ground floor on the east, west and north sides until 1939.

The Town House was renovated in 1985 and floodlit to mark its 250th anniversary, a fitting tribute to a building that has seen many exciting events, such as the visit by Wellington in 1827, when it is believed the town's Halberd was presented in recognition of its efforts during the Napoleonic Wars.

It was in this building on the 18th September 1810 that Leonard Raisbeck, Recorder of Stockton, first moved the idea of a railway or canal between the port of Stockton and the surrounding area. A plaque in the Council Chamber, commemorates this speech. In the following years, great civic dinners were held to celebrate, firstly the laying of the first tracks of the S&D in 1822 at St. John's Well and then the official opening itself in 1825 as well as subsequent anniversaries.

There was once a covered cross in the market place but this was removed in 1768 when the Doric Column was seento be more in keeping with the splendour of the Town house; the town's stocks and whipping post also stood here. As trade expanded in the late 17th century the shambles — butchers' shops — were built in 1699; the present building, now an indoor market area, dates from 1825.

Continue along the High Street as far as the Swallow Hotel

Stockton Manor House (Castle)

Stockton's medieval Manor House — or Castle — was sited where the Swallow Hotel now stands, and in the late Middle Ages it provided a fortified base for the Prince Bishops of Durham, who owned the House until 1640. It was later overrun by the Scots in the Civil War, and destroyed by order of the Commonwealth Government in 1652. Remains from the stone work can still be seen in several of the older buildings.

Stockton Castle

Continue along the High Street until the junction with Wharf Street . Turn left here to cross at the pedestrian traffic lights.

The Port of Stockton

The name "Wharf Street" recalls the large areas of wharfs and staithes that made up the Port of Stockton. Sadly, recent development, most particularly the new relief road, has eliminated almost all signs of the old dock area.

As the River Tees gradually silted up from Tudor times onwards, Stockton gradually assumed greater importance as a port, at the expense of Yarm higher up the river. It became the main trading port for South Durham, Cumberland, Westmorland and the North Riding of Yorkshire, exporting butter, cheese, bacon, flour, corn from the lower Durham and Yorkshire Dales, and lead from the Swaledale, Weardale and Teesdale mines. Wood was imported from the Baltic and later coal from Newcastle and Sunderland for both domestic and industrial use, and to fuel the town's gas works which were established in 1822.

Stockton's expansion as a port was severely handicapped because of the winding nature of the River Tees, particularly when larger vessels came into use. For this reason, in 1810, the river was straightened by a new cut or "navigation" between Stockton and Portrack, shortening the distance to the sea by over two miles by cutting out a tight bend in the river. The course of the old river can still be traced at the far side of the Tees by the old race course.

Stockton shipyards around 1904

Turn right and then left at the roundabout. Opposite the supermarket, cross the main road at the traffic lights to the little group of buildings opposite. Look at the small, squat house on the right, 48 Bridge Road.

48 Bridge Road and the Beginning of the Railway

There are two plaques here. One, on the high wall a short distance to the right, commemorates the laying of the first section of railway track near this spot by Thomas Meynell on 23rd May 1822. The second on the wall of 48 Bridge Road claims that the building was the world's first ticket office.

Courtesy of The Northern Echo

St John's Crossing, 1925

The first claim is undoubtedly true, though the actual point where the first rail was laid was a few yards to the north east under the tarmac of the busy road where there was once the level crossing at St. John's Well.

Although the second claim has not been validated, it is true that the building does pre-date the Stockton and Darlington Railway. Tickets, probably coal yard receipts, were issued from the small office in later years. Note the site of the round clock which used to adorn the wall of the building.

Inns were in fact the first ticket offices for the Stockton and Darlington Railway, following standard stage coach practice which used them as departure and booking points. Sadly, none of the old inns in central Stockton, from where the first tickets were sold, have survived.

The first actual station in Stockton was a small wooden building without a platform, by a siding just off Bridge Road, which was soon replaced by a more ample stone construction some 40 yards to the north west on the other side of Bridge Road. When the Middlesbrough extension was built in 1830 and South Stockton opened in 1836, this station soon fell into disuse and was closed.

48 Bridge Road today

The level crossing here had its own small signal box and signals, and survived until the 1960s, the line to the staithes going through what is now the supermarket.

The area behind the buildings where the line of tracks can still be seen was part of the once important Stockton South Goods Yard with several sidings, a large warehouse, coal drops and a lime siding.

Recross the road, go across the supermarket car park, turning right to the riverbank and pick up a paved path beyond the shrubbery which runs along the riverside.

Victoria Bridge and Thornaby Station

Look right to the handsome road bridge over the Tees. Victoria bridge, pictured above, was built in 1887 to commemorate Queen Victoria's Golden Jubilee. Thornaby Station, nearby, originally known as South Stockton, was transferred to its present site from a point closer to the river to make room for the bridge.

Follow the path downriver past the supermarket

Mellanby Shipyard

The site of the present supermarket was once a large shipbuilders' yard — Mellanby Shipyard (1826). On the opposite bank was Craig Taylors (1884). Shipbuilding was an important Stockton industry. Among the 20th century landscaping it is hard to visualise an entire waterfront heaving with shipyards, rail sidings, docks and warehouses.

Continue along the riverside path, going through a wrought iron gateway, straight ahead to Castlegate Warehouse.

Castlegate Warehouse

The Castlegate Warehouse is the only building along this part of the riverside to survive from Stockton and Darlington Railway times but is typical of the many warehouses which once occupied the whole riverside area. It has been beautifully restored as an office and leisure centre. It is well worth visiting its coffee-shop and bar on the second floor, if only to enjoy the panoramic views of the riverside — and to muse on what it once was like.

The original railway used to follow the quay, along which there were four sets of coal staithes, which in effect were wooden jetties along the river edge from which the wagons deposited their loads directly into the holds of the ships waiting below. The earliest of these staithes were designed by Timothy Hackworth, the great S&D locomotive engineer.

All along this stretch of river were

Courtesy of The Northern Echo

The old S&D railway wharfs with Castlegate Warehouse in the background

inns and taverns, once full of dockers, sailors, and railway, shipyard and other workers. At inns like the Fleece and the Black Lion tickets for the railway could be bought. In the early years of the line, travel was sub-contracted out to private operators who ran their own private horse drawn carriages along the rails, with names like *Defence* or the *Union*. Notice the anchor and the surviving bollard by the path where large vessels would have been moored.

Continue past Castlegate, bearing right to rejoin the riverside path. Cross by the footbridge, turn left along Riverside and then right into the lower part of Finkle Street.

Finkle Street

On the corner of Finkle Street (now the spiral ramp to the Castle Centre roof car park) was the Customs House Tavern which also sold railway tickets. Close by here was Martins Wharf, the main freight trans-shipment wharf from the railway. The Green Dragon side of Finkle Street remains unspoilt, and contains one of the oldest houses in Stockton— now a cafe.

Turn left up Finkle Street, right through the alley into Green Dragon Yard back to the Information Centre.

The oldest house in Stockton

PART TWO
Out of Stockton

This part of the Trail explores areas outside Stockton Town Centre which have particularly strong associations with the early history of the Stockton & Darlington Railway.

Thornaby to Preston-on-Tees

Preston Park is easily reached by taking the A135 Yarm Road from Stockton. Follow the brown tourist signs to Preston Hall Park, turning sharp left into the park entrance to the car park. Public transport users can either catch any Yarm bus from the High Street which will pass Preston Park entrance, or catch a train from Stockton or Thornaby Stations to Eaglescliffe.

The rail journey from Thornaby crosses the impressive Tees Bridge which replaced the world's first railway suspension bridge designed by Captain Samuel Brown in 1830. It was a lightweight structure and proved unable to cope with heavy traffic and had to be replaced by a conventional structure in 1844.

Preston Park

From Eaglescliffe Station it is about a mile's walk to Preston Park. Follow Station Road to the main road junction, cross and turn left. At the edge of the park a wooden stile-gate on the right gives access to a footpath alongside the main road between the trees — this is the original line of trackbed of the Stockton and Darlington Railway. One of the passing loops of this single track line was situated in the vicinity. In the early years of operation, the first train or coach to pass a marker post at either side of the loop was given priority at the loop — a system which led to frequent arguments!

Preston Hall

It was almost certainly somewhere along this section of track that the famous race noted by eyewitnesses took place between *Locomotion* and its train and a coach on the parallel road, as immortalised by the famous painting by Terence Cuneo *(see cover)*. When the Leeds Northern Railway was built parallel to the S&D, on the west side of the A135, in1852, the route through Preston Park was soon abandoned for what is now the present BR line to Stockton and Thornaby.

Preston Hall is almost an exact contemporary of the S&D Railway, being built in 1825 by David Burton Fowler — the handsome conservatory was added later.

It is now a magnificent museum and country park. The collections include period rooms and costume, armour, paintings (including the famous De la Tour *Dice Players*) and a carefully reconstructed street full of Victorian shops and workshops. Refreshments are available. Future plans include an ambitious scheme to restore part of the Stockton and Darlington Railway with a replica contemporary steam engine.

Yarm

Yarm is easily reached a further three miles along the A135 — disc parking is available in the High Street. Public transport users have a choice of frequent buses either direct from Stockton or from outside Preston Park.

Rail users with a historical bent might like to take the train from either Thornaby or Eaglescliffe to Allens West Station which was originally built for the Admiralty but opened to the public in 1970. Allens West stands close by the site of the original Yarm Station, a horse drawn carriage service taking passengers into Yarm, a distance of just over a mile. Today's rail users have to walk!

On the Yarm-Darlington road, just before the Cleveland Bay Inn, is a surviving building which was originally an agent's house and coal depot on the long vanished S&D freight branch into Yarm. An S&D plaque "D13" high on the wall

Aerial view of Yarm

Dennis Wompra, Middlesbrough

indicates its S&D origins. The numbering is from east to west across the S&D rail system as it existed in 1856-60. Note also the

The 'D13' building

painted up windows.

Yarm, bounded on three sides by the River Tees, is a lovely old town to explore, with narrow wynds, riverside walks, a magnificent Parish Church. Though Norman in parts, this largely dates from the 18th century. There is also a rare early Methodist octagonal chapel of 1763 which John Wesley claimed was one of the most elegant in England.

The ancient bridge over the Tees, still carrying the main road, dates

Yarm Wesleyan Chapel

from 1400 when Bishop Skirlaw of Durham ordered its construction. Its northern arch was replaced by a draw bridge during the Civil War to hold back the Scots — if you look carefully you will still see how that arch differs from the others where it was rebuilt in the 18th century.

The town's charter goes back to the time of King John in 1207 who granted a weekly market and two annual fairs — an indication of the town's importance at that time. In the 18th and 19th centuries an amazing range of industries flourished here — brewing, clockmaking, tanning, papermaking, ropemaking and ship building and

Yarm Bridge

the manufacture of barrels and nails. Elegant Georgian merchant houses built on the prosperity of that industry still dominate the town. There are several fine old coaching inns, including the 300 year old Ketton Ox, as Yarm, like Stockton, was on several important 18th and early 19th century stage coach routes.

Also like Stockton, Yarm was once a sizeable port, exporting farm produce and lead and bringing in coal and other products, ships coming up the winding, tidal river to avoid the inhospitable salt flats and marshes which are now Middlesbrough and Billingham. The town remained an important port until the mid 18th century when its trade was increasingly overtaken by Stockton. Improved turnpike roads and the new railways totally destroyed the river trade, and Yarm became a peaceful backwater. Consequently it has remained an essentially Georgian town, not unlike Stockton used to be before the Stockton & Darlington Railway triggered off such a period of rapid growth and change.

A detailed guide to Yarm, *The Yarm Trail*, published by Stockton Council, is available at Stockton Information Centre and Preston Park Museum.

Ironically, a railway does still dominate the town, the spectacular 760 yard long Yarm Viaduct with two skew arches over the River Tees and 41 smaller ones through the town itself, dividing even the church from the town centre. Built by Thomas Grainger and John Bourne in 1852 for the Leeds Northern Railway and requiring an estimated seven million bricks to construct, it still carries the massive freight trains serving the industry of Teesside and Tyneside, though Yarm's station has long closed and passenger trains rarely operate over the line.

Two buildings are of special interest for the S & D Railway. The first of these is the George and Dragon Inn in the High Street where, on February 12, 1820 a group of Yarm businessmen met in the Commercial Room to pursue the building of the Stockton & Darlington Railway, Mr Thomas Meynell, the Squire of Yarm, presiding — a plaque marks the event.

The second is the little Town Hall which dates from 1710 when it was built by the Third Viscount Fauconberg, Lord of the Manor, as a courthouse and market hall.

A plaque on the wall commemorates the names of the five promoters and pioneers from Yarm who have linked their names and that of the town of Yarm with that ambitious and challenging enterprise: Thomas Meynell (Chairman), Benjamin Flounders, Jeremy Cairn, Richard Miles, Thomas Miles.

Fighting Cocks

Though the Fighting Cocks Inn is just a short way across the Stockton Borough boundary, it is an important and relatively unspoilt Stockton and Darlington site which has changed little in appearance over the last 160 years.

To get there, motorists should take the A67 from Yarm or from Eaglescliffe towards Darlington to Dinsdale, where about half a mile north of Dinsdale Station, on the corner of the Sedberge road, is the Fighting Cocks.

Public transport users can best catch the Heritage Line train from Thornaby, Eaglescliffe or Allen West to Dinsdale and walk about half a mile through the town to the Fighting Cocks.

Between Allens West and a point about half a mile east of Dinsdale, rail travellers have the satisfaction of knowing that they are travelling along part of the original line of the Stockton and Darlington Railway.

The original Stockton and Darlington route branched off before Dinsdale heading towards North Road Station at Darlington and then on to Shildon and beyond the coal mines at Winston, via stationary engine-hauled inclines at Brusselton and Etherley. It ran immediately behind the Fighting Cocks Inn over a level crossing. Part of the track, with a somewhat forlornly optimistic "Distance" signal, still survives at time of writing as a freight siding, as does the later S&D Fighting Cocks Station (closed in 1887 when Dinsdale Station was opened) which is now a private house.

Illustrated London News

Fighting Cocks Station — the way it used to be

Passengers could alight from what originally were horse-drawn coaches at any convenient point along the railway (platforms being a later luxury). This inn and level crossing was such a point, where tickets could be issued and refreshment taken whilst waiting for a train. Refreshments are still available even though the trains are no more.

The Fighting Cocks Inn has changed relatively little in appearance since the days when rail passengers purchased their tickets there; it is, therefore, arguably the oldest railway ticket sales office still in existence!

The Fighting Cocks

To complete your exploration of early Stockton and Darlington Rail Heritage be sure to visit **Darlington Railway Centre and Museum** at North Road Station, Darlington, easily reached by direct train on BR's Heritage Line or by the A167 main road out of Darlington town centre, where you'll find George Stephenson's original *Locomotion* (1825), Hackworth's *Derwent* (1845) and an early S&D coach, among many other treasures of early North East Railway history. *Tel 0325 460532 for opening times and other information.* **The Timothy Hackworth Museum** at Shildon is situated in the great locomotive engineer's former home at Soho Cottages, Shildon, close to the site of the works where such famous engines as *Sans Pareil* and *Royal George* were built. There is a short rail trail nearby. *For information ring 0388 816166 ext. 4290 (weekdays) or 0388 777464 weekends and evenings.*